What Would Shakespeare Say?
Hamlet's Words, Words, Words.

Ben Nelson

Illustrations by:

Alex Kleider

Ben Nelson

Paul Nelson

www.whatwouldshakespearesay.com

Copyright © 2013 Ben Nelson
Author: Ben Nelson
Illustrations: Alex Kleider and Paul Nelson

ISBN-13: 978-1491234365
ISBN-10: 1491234369

To Louis and Jessica; words aren't really that important between us, nor will they ever be.

To my family with thanks and apologies.

For Harold C Goddard; we know what we are...

And of course, to William Shakespeare:

A hundred hours I spend in here
learn Petrarch, Chaucer, and Shakespeare.
So many words to say on so many thoughts
I count them o'er, my mind is wrought;
I cannot see the forest for the trees
70,000 words are known and of these
98% comprehension is needed in context
to understand: no why I'm so sorely vexed.
I doubt great authors intended this
That our understanding, so hit or miss,
Should prevent them sharing thoughts with us
That we should read, seethe, groan and cuss.
A great mystery, always, your works for me
A greater frustration, Shakespeare, for thee
-Nelson, 2003

CONTENTS

Ben Nelson

How to Use This Book

This book is intended for those of us who want to make the greatest words ever written part of our lives, but is just as much a tool in understanding Shakespeare. It has a table of contents guiding you to iconic passages worth knowing by heart, and practice quizzes to sharpen your skill in quoting Shakespeare. Each quote has a description of its context, meaning, and relevance in the play. This is to shield you from being just a bluffer; not only will you know what Shakespeare would say, but you will know why Shakespeare said it.

Remember, "Reading maketh a full man (but) conference maketh a ready man." Want to be ready? Practice these quotes. Practice in your head, in this book, on your friends, at the movies, on the bus, at work, etc. so that when you really need a brilliant quote to silence a critic or sum up a moment, you are the ready woman or man. Use this book, learn the quotes, make them a part of your world, and share that world with people around you. Great words, like great ideas, are worth sharing, especially if they make you great too.

Ben Nelson

Most notable Quotes

What Would Shakespeare Say?

Introduction

Ahh, Hamlet. For many, it is the highlight of all English Literature; it is not just a play, but "The Play." Amongst academics, few plays can arouse as much interest and debate as this play about the Prince of Denmark. Amongst the rest of us, it arouses confusion. Was he really mad? Did he really love Ophelia? What does he mean "To be"? Does Hamlet not kill the king because he is scared, passive, out of shape, too philosophical, or because he doesn't believe his father's ghost? It is a play of questions. Of course, none of these questions make sense without some background of the story.

Hamlet's father has died (a "murder most foul", as it turns out to be), and there is "something rotten" in the state of Denmark. A ghost has appeared several times, and it looks like Hamlet's father, so naturally Hamlet confronts the ghost. The ghost claims to be his father and tells Hamlet he has been murdered by his brother, Claudius, who is now married to Hamlet's mother, Gertrude. In other words, Hamlet's father was murdered by his Uncle, who then married his mother. Hamlet then

spends the play feigning insanity to test this
story from the ghost. While doing so, he drives
Ophelia, his occasional lover, crazy, and stages
a very conspicuous play to test if Claudius is
the murderer.

The play does the trick, but Hamlet
hesitates to kill Claudius despite being ready to
"drink hot blood." However, he does kill
Polonius, a counsellor to the king, and shortly
after this Ophelia drowns herself. Hamlet and
his best friend Horatio then debate with a
gravedigger, and Hamlet agrees to duel with
Ophelia's brother, Laertes. He apologizes to
Laertes before the duel, which must throw
Laertes for a loop as he and Claudius are
planning on poisoning Hamlet. During the
duel, Gertrude and Laertes are poisoned, and
Laertes reveals Claudius is behind it all.
Hamlet then kills Claudius before dying from
the poison himself. As he dies, Fortinbras, a
fellow ruler, comes to the grisly scene and
orders Hamlet's body borne out in honour; he
also mentions he may be taking the throne from
Hamlet's family, but Horatio may have
something to say about that. It is clear that
people have been killed, but it is not clear if the
killing will end. The glory of thrones, the

validity of titles, and the purpose of the play all depend on a person's perspective.

Everyone will see the same action, but not as much of the same meaning in this play. This is because we see ourselves; should Hamlet exact revenge on the king, or not? Would I? Is his mother wrong to marry Claudius, or not? Is he afraid to murder, or too moral to do so? Would I murder my uncle? Is he a lazy philosopher or a passionate artist? What am I? All these questions pose themselves in a deep discussion and academic reading of the play. In a short book about it, one can only say that Hamlet has a meaning for anyone with a moral conundrum, a passion for life, or who has ever thought about death. In the words of Harold C Goddard:

> There is no mystery in a looking glass (mirror) until someone looks into it. Then, though it remains the same glass, it presents a different face to each man who holds it in front of him. The same is true of a work of art... However much we all see in common in such a work, at the center we behold a fragment of our own soul, and the greater the art the greater the fragment. *Hamlet* is possibly the most convincing example in existence of this truth.
> (The Meaning of Shakespeare; Volume 1, pp 331)

The mirror of Hamlet magnifies the appearing and the doubting by raising the stakes to a man either being a king or being nothing. For many, there are things you just need to do; Hamlet should be king, he should avenge his father's death, he should be a murderer, yet he is not and does not. It seems so obvious a choice, yet he doubts. Hamlet is exceptional because we tend to doubt with him, and not against him; his problems become our problems. This play, like any great piece of work, poses questions that we need to find answers for ourselves.

Regardless of the answers we find, there are things worth noting, and the mirror of Hamlet is there to be examined by each of us. So here are the best glimpses into the mirror, glimpses you can use to help clarify or distort the reality that surrounds you. Ultimately you are going to decide how these quotes are to be, or not to be, taken. And "there's the rub".

Ben Nelson

The Quotes

1) A little more than kin and less than kind
    1.2.65.

"Closer than family and yet less than civil to each other" is Hamlet's pointed barb for Claudius, summing up the relationship between the two of them. It has a double meaning as do most of the quotes in Shakespeare's plays. It can be used to show someone is closer to you than your family even though they are just a friend, or that your family is not as kind to you as they should be, or are less kind than your kind friends. This is a useful quote for any occasion when your family refuses to do something nice for you. It is also very helpful when your kids misbehave, your parents chastise you, or your close friends are closer to you than your family and you'd like them to know it.

2)   All that lives must die,
     passing through nature to eternity.
     1.2.72-73.

"Everything that lives will die and leave our natural world." This quote can be taken at face value. Claudius is trying to console Hamlet regarding the death of his father. Yes, you are allowed to pronounce "eternity" as "e-ter-ni-tie." Imperfect rhymes are common in Shakespeare, and if it looks like it should rhyme, often we bend the pronunciation to suit. Shakespeare spelled his name at least ten different ways in his life, so why worry too much about something as trite as pronunciation? You can gently use this at a funeral and find some solace in it. However, if you feel like having a laugh, broadcast it at a turkey dinner or a fishing derby.

3)   To persevere
in obstinate condolement is a course
of impious stubbornness.
1.2.92-94.

"To follow this course of action is a stupid, stubborn idea." Here Claudius is chastising Hamlet for his continued grief at his father's death, and maybe Claudius feels threatened because he shows so little grief himself. It could be a call to optimism for anyone stuck in a depressed state, or a reprimand for anyone gambling too much, as in "you may or may not have a feeling about that number, but betting your life savings on it is not a good idea." It also applies to anyone doing something unnatural, such as them dying their hair or getting cosmetic surgery.

4)   I know not seems.
      1.2.76.

"I am not pretending." Hamlet uses this
quote to describe his disposition after his
father's death. Hamlet *is* upset, he does not just
seem upset, and this is a prediction of what will
come in the play; characters will be themselves,
but they will often seem to be someone else.
Almost every conflict in the play is based upon
this same premise. If you note all of the times
appearance of what is and the reality behind
that appearance are a problem, you will have a
very close reading of the text. Being and
seeming, the hidden side of characters, is what
Shakespeare brought to life on stage and a chief
reason for his enduring popularity. His
characters are real to us because they are so
complex and have such strength in their hidden
personality. This is a spiteful comment to
anyone who accuses you of feigning your
disposition or political position. Of course, it is
also cleverly used anytime you pick up a
needle, as in "I know not *seams*."

"I know not *seems.*"

5) Tis unmanly grief;
it shows a will most incorrect to heaven
1.2.94-95.

"You are being womanly in your grief. Stop it. God made you a man." This chastisement is similar to quote 3 above, but reflects some stereotypes of manliness and womanliness, and is an attempt by Claudius to get at the pride of Hamlet. It is a poignant spur to turn an over-emotional man into a stouter example of masculinity. It is also great for anyone crying over spilt milk or being too upset over a trivial matter.

6) 'Tis an unweeded garden,
that grows to seed; things rank and
gross in nature possess it merely.
1.2.135-137.

"This is a mess, and it grows messier. Dirty, foul things have overrun it." This quote can be fruitfully applied to any home gardening or planting project, although in the play it is being applied to the State of Denmark. Hamlet is disgusted with the way the world is turning out to be; in the garden of Denmark not only are disgusting things growing up and overcoming the goodness around them, it is getting ready for even further corruption and grossness in the generation to come. The allusion to any state or congregation overwhelmed with scum holds fast today. This quote is not recommended for use on teenage girls and their hair without you being ready for some serious consequences. However, it is useful when discussing politics, a poorly run daycare, or any general collection you would rather not be a part of.

"O, that this too, too solid flesh would melt, thaw, and resolve itself into a dew!"

7)   O, that this too too solid flesh would
      melt, thaw, and resolve itself into a
      dew!
      1.2.129-130.

"I wish my body would melt into liquid and then into a vapour" literally, but figuratively it may be taken as meaning "I wish I could disappear." Hamlet is referring to his body, which some literature buffs think was rather portly. He wishes to be free of life bound in a body, and this is a solid (pun intended) expression of depression. This is bound to come in handy any time you make a mistake, wish you could disappear, but have an audience who won't let you. It is a perfect slogan for *The Biggest Loser,* or a quick-witted way to acknowledge embarrassment and guilt whenever you get caught with your pants down; I'm sure Bill Clinton had this in mind after Lewinsky-gate. It is also an excellent quote to use as you eat that last mouthful of *Ben and Jerry's,* or a jab before you wash away the remnants of a snowman with a hose.

8)   As if increase of appetite had grown
     by what it fed on
     1.2.144-145.

"It's as though hunger has increased by what it has eaten." This is a great description of a dog at his dinner bowl, but Hamlet is describing how his mother originally seemed to love his father. In his mind, the wheels of what happened to his father are beginning to turn and his suspicion is growing. Gertrude was so in love with Hamlet's late father that it seemed the more time and love they shared together, the more her love for him would grow, even by the same amount. Barry White was not far off with his song *I Can't Get Enough of Your Love, Babe.* His exact words were "The more you give the more I want." This quote by Shakespeare or White, if you prefer a modern twist, can apply to anyone with an increasing energy for their passion in life, such as lovers, workaholics or selfish gold-diggers. You could also use it to describe a baby who won't quit nursing or a game of *Hungry Hungry Hippos.*

"As if increase of appetite had grown
by what it fed on"

9) Was a man, take him for all in all,
    I shall not look upon his like again.
    1.2.187-188.

"He was a typical man really, (or he was a paragon of men different from any other), but not to be repeated in any other man when you consider everything he was." Hamlet here is grieving the death and loss of his father, but how sad is he? His father was a man and, good or bad, Hamlet won't see him again. Was his father an amazing human, or just another amazing human? Really, this quote is existentialism at its finest—we are all nothing yet uniquely amazing at the same time. A great tribute to any friend or family member, and a sarcastic send off for would be suitors or past boyfriends.

10) Foul deeds will rise, though all the earth
     o'erwhelm them, to men's eyes.
     1.2.257-258.

"The truth of bad deeds will come out, regardless of how much dirt we try to cover them with." Perhaps Hamlet the character believed in karma, as here the statement is that the guilty will never be free from their foul deeds. Perhaps he is just commenting on his father's ghost arising to push him to action. Perhaps it is neither. Want to instil guilt or fear in someone? Here is a quote to get the guilt started, although my parents did a great job without it. Use this whenever someone thinks they have gotten away with something, or when you have been wounded with impunity.

11) Keep you in the rear of your affection, out of the shot and danger of desire. 1.3.34-35.

"Control your emotions before they overtake you." This quote is Polonius chastising his daughter, Ophelia, suggesting she keep her attraction for Hamlet in check. It is a pretty common warning of parents to youth in their hormone driven years. "Hold your horses" or, "Keep it in your pants" say almost the same thing, but not quite so eloquently. True and applicable today, and well suited for gluttons, drunks, and pushy suitors.

12) The chariest maid is prodigal enough if she unmask her beauty to the moon. 1.3.36-37.

"Even the most modest woman is productive (or re-productive) enough if she gets naked in front of the moon." Nature appreciates art and beauty, so who needs an audience? This quote from Polonius is a nice way of suggesting some modesty in dress and decorum to anyone you care about. I've always found this to be a stupid idea, because by this logic the greatest treasures are never found, but waste away to dust without appreciation. Of course I don't have a daughter, and am sure I will appreciate this quote more when I do.

13) Virtue itself 'scapes not calumnious strokes.
1.3.38.

"Even the noblest among us are in danger of disaster" or, "Just because you are a great person, it doesn't mean bad things won't happen to you." This is an especially true sentiment during times of tyrants and dictators, and apparently Polonius, the speaker of this quote, knows a lot about both of them. It is a suitable sentiment to console those who have bad luck, whether in gambling, relationships, or bowling.

14) Youth to itself rebels.
1.3.44.

"Youth fights against itself." This is a classic quote about the futility of trying to understand teenagers and is very helpful counsel for parents. It is the essential rebuttal to the sentiment of James Dean. "What are you rebelling against?" met by his "What have you got?" is now countered by this quote from

Hamlet, a more legitimately troubled youth. Whoever they are, the youth never knows why they rebel; they just rebel because it is what they do. If ever a teenager tells you to butt out, just fire this at them and watch the wheels turn in confusion. They will be trying to come up with a reply long after you have forgotten you said it.

15) Those friends thou hast, and their adoption tried, grapple them to thy soul with hoops of steel.
1.3.62-63.

"Keep your friends who have been tested close to you." If one plays up the image of "adoption," this applies to any parent who refuses to "cut the cord." They have grappled their kids to their sides with hoops of steel. You will probably want to keep this quote handy as your children grow and get ready to make the mistakes we all do. Also, this is good advice for anyone embarking on a journey, as in this context of Polonius to his son Laertes, or for youth passing into adulthood.

16) Beware of entrance to a quarrel; but, being in, bear't that th' opposed may beware of thee.
1.3.65-67.

"Try not to pick a fight, but if you do fight, make your opposition regret it." Polonius here offers some advice to his son, Laertes, before Laertes heads away for education and growth into adulthood. If it seems like these pieces of advice from Polonius go on and on, it is because they do. What parent doesn't overdo it when they drop off their son or daughter for their new life at college? This over advising also points to another of the key themes in the play; the effect of parents on their children. Polonius advises Laertes and Ophelia, and Hamlet's father's ghost advises him, both to terrible ends. This is an oath worth pondering before engaging in a conflict. As well, this sentiment is heavily used in politics and family quarrels, and is a priceless threat for anyone playing a game of Risk.

17) This above all- to thine own self be true, and it must follow, as the night the day, thou canst not then be false to any man.
1.3.78-80.

"If you are honest with yourself, you will be honest with others as well." Yet another ironic statement from Polonius when so much in this play is focussed on deception and appearance. This is useful to encourage honesty in daily life, and a hopeful prayer for anyone questioning the validity of jewelry they have purchased. If gems are true to themselves, they will not be deceiving to you either, but will be genuine treasures. By and far it is most useful to remind people that they should trust their instincts, and just be honest with themselves. If we can be genuine and honest, a disposition hardly found in this play, we will avoid many of the problems frequently found in this play. To quote Sir Walter Scott, "Oh what a tangled web we weave when we practice to deceive." This quote says don't bother trying to weave in the first place, and your life will be a lot happier.

"To thine own self be true"

18) The apparel oft proclaims the man
1.3.72.

"The clothes make the man." Use this quote whenever you receive a compliment on your apparel or when you get a friend to dress up for a special occasion, job interview, or date. And of course be sure to use it when you see an Elvis impersonator, or someone proud of who they are, regardless of what other people may say, as in the illustration. Your clothes speak loud and clear about what you are, so embrace them and enjoy it. You should also remember that you are supposed to dress for the job you want, so you may as well let your clothing proclaim your self-love or they will proclaim your self-neglect. Want to be a success? Dress like one, a key aspect of the sociological perspective of symbolic interactionism. A more sinister application is finding lipstick on a man's collar, a bold proclamation by his apparel indeed.

"The apparel oft proclaims the man"

"Neither a borrower nor a lender be"

19) Neither a borrower nor a lender be
     for loan oft loses both itself and friend,
     and borrowing dulls the edge of
     husbandry.
     1.3.75-77.

"Don't lend money to a friend; you lose your friend and the money you leant. And don't borrow it either-- it will prevent you from being thrifty." That's right, even more advice from Polonius. Is it any wonder he was instructed to speak with "more matter, less art" as in "get on with it?" This quote is a good way to prevent a friend borrowing any sum of money, small or large, from you. It makes it easy to say no while deflecting serious contention away from yourself, and is a wise chastisement if you feel the need to borrow from a friend.

20) When the blood burns, how prodigal
     the soul lends the tongue vows.
     1.3.116-117.

"It's easy to say things you don't mean when you are emotional," although in this context of Polonius to his daughter, it is more similar to "men will say anything to get into a woman's pants." This is still true today, and is effective in many different contexts. Have you ever heard a friend swear "that's the last time I ever _____?" Say this instead of "heard that one before" and you'll draw some noteworthy attention.

21) It is a custom more honour'd in the breach than in the observance. 1.4.15-16.

"People tend more to not do it than to do it," be "it" loving your mother in law, voting, paying full taxes, or properly observing Lent. This is easily applied to many modern customs, traditions, and political campaign promises. Is someone bothering you about going over the speed limit when you drive? Here is a resounding reply that ensures no more backseat drivers giving you advice.

22) I do not set my life at a pin's fee. 1.4.65.

"I don't value my life as more than a pin." Hamlet states here that he cares so little for his life because of his misery that it is worth only the price of a pin. So, he resolves himself to pursue his father's ghost to ask it questions; he must know the truth! You may find some abstract chances to use this quote, such as when you are being told to pay up or else, or when you have bill collectors call you about unpaid parking tickets. You will probably also use this as a battle cry for the hopeless or as a taunt when entering a quarrel, as in "Bring it on, I've got nothing to lose."

23) Nature cannot choose his origin.
1.4.26.

"We can't help what we are" or "I am as God made me." Hamlet here is philosophizing while waiting to see if his father's ghost really is haunting Denmark. He has to wait and see; he can't help it. What it means out of context is that you cannot help who or what you are or where you come from. There is an ongoing debate between psychologists about what is more important; nature, how you were when you were born, or nurture, the way you were raised. This comment squarely places the onus of personality on nature, and states that whatever you may do wrong, it is not your fault, but the fault of your genes. Use it to excuse anything bad that you ever do, get caught doing, or have ever done. In addition, you can use it as an excuse for the behaviour of others, such as your dog or child doing his business on your neighbour's lawn.

"Nature cannot choose his origin."

24) Murder most foul, as in the best it is
1.5.27.

This is always a popular quote when the media discusses murder cases. "Murder is horrendous, even in the best murders" although there may be a double meaning in this quote. It may also mean that murder is the best when it is foul; if you are going to commit murder, you may as well do a good job of making it the most terrible type of murder you can. This is a poignant quote when discussing avian flu, *Duck Hunt* or when suspicious of Mrs. Peacock while playing *Clue*.

"Murder most foul"

25) There are more things in heaven and
     Earth, Horatio, than are dreamt of in
     your philosophy.
     1.5.166-167.

"Dream as you can, you philosophers (or
scientists) will never imagine all of the
possibilities of what is or could be." The
humanist versus the rationalist! Here Hamlet is
replying to Horatio regarding the validity of his
father's ghost, and how it has appeared to him.
If philosophy cannot even "dream" of what
there could be in the world, how hopeless is it
in dealing with emotions or the unexplained?
On a deeper level this quote could mean that
knowledge will never be as powerful as
imagination, as Albert Einstein said. It is
surprising this quote was never a slogan for *Dr.
Who* or *The X-Files*, but the sentiment survives
today thanks in part to conspiracy theorists.
This quote is great when explaining foolish
mistakes, UFO's, unnecessary shopping sprees,
or the Ikea catalogue.

"There are more things in heaven and earth, Horatio, than are dreamt of in your philosophy."

26) Such wanton, wild, and usual slips
as are companions noted and most
known to youth and liberty.
2.1.22-24.

"This behaviour is usually what you
find in young people." Here Polonius makes
a surprisingly astute observation of young
people, and in particular, of Hamlet. This is
a great quote for anyone immature, childish,
or foolish.

27)   More matter, with less art.
2.2.98

"Get to the point" or in a more general context,
"Less style, more substance," is Gertrude's
message to Polonius as he drags on and on
about whether or not Hamlet is mad. How
many times have you wanted to tell someone to
get on with it, but did not want to come across
as impatient? Now you can say it with a smile
and expect less resistance, but your point will
have been well and humorously made.

"Such wanton, wild, and usual slips
as are companions noted and most
known to youth and liberty."

28) By heaven, it is as proper to our age
to cast beyond ourselves in our
opinions as it is common for the
younger sort to lack discretion.
2.1.114-118.

"We the aged and old give our opinions to
everyone, as much as young people make
mistakes. It's what we are meant to do." This is
Polonius again; how can so much wisdom come
from someone who is so oblivious about his
own life? He is speaking of the elderly in this
sentiment. This is related to the preceding
quote about youth, and is a wonderful
explanation of why the elderly have so many
opinions about everything, or why they insist
on driving long after they should. This is great
to use whenever you want to do something just
because, or when your age doesn't recommend
you do it, but you do it anyways. It is even
more useful when you want to tell someone else
what to do, but don't really have a frame of
reference to do so. Regardless, use it as a
reminder to cast beyond yourself, think big, and
take that chance you feel you could get away
with!

29) Doubt thou the stars are fire;
    Doubt that the sun doth move;
    Doubt truth to be a liar;
    But never doubt I love.
    2.2.116-119.

    "Doubt everything you know is true, even things that must be true, but never doubt that I love you." If you need a cliché for a lover, use this one. The trouble is this quote is from a letter from Hamlet to Ophelia when he is feigning insanity. More troublesome for interpretation of it in the context of the play is that perhaps he does mean it, as he later takes her death so hard. Perhaps he is just playing Ophelia to test her loyalty, or using her to strengthen the validity of his insane acting. Use it as a quick response to an insecure lover, but not if they have read their Hamlet. Then it reeks of sarcasm, dishonesty, and usury.

30) To be honest, as this world goes,
    is to be one man pick'd out of ten
    thousand.
    2.2.178-179.

"It's about one in ten thousand that you
find someone who really is honest." Hamlet is
confronted by Polonius, and so decides to have
a go at him. This is a disheartening quote, but
worth feeding to a judge, lawyer, or police
officer if they ask you "Why did you do it?" If
they are really quick, they will understand your
barb; if not, you can smile, knowing that good
learning is about as common as honesty.

31) Though this be madness, yet there is
    method in't.
    2.2.206.

"Though this is crazy, there is a purpose
in it." One of Shakespeare's most famous
quotes! It is amazing that Polonius is insightful
enough to know that Hamlet is trying to seem
crazy, and that Hamlet actually is not crazy.
And if that is what Polonius thinks, most

thespians think he is right. Often our gut instinct tells us what we can't quite rationally figure out. This quote is perfect for anyone having a temper tantrum, (yes, even babies) and for those who fake small amounts of madness to get their way, such as terrible method actors.

32) There is nothing either good or bad, but thinking makes it so.
2.2.253-254.

"Things are just bad because we think they are." Do we make a meaning for everything? Are right and wrong actual things or just our perspective on things? If Darwinism as a social perspective is true, then this idea has validity. But perhaps it is not, and perhaps there are morals and values beyond our human meaning of them. Animal research into fairness has recently suggested this using two caged monkeys; get each one to give you a rock, and then give one a grape and one a piece of cucumber as a reward. Amazingly, the one with the cucumber is jealous. If you believe morals are simply made up rules, then ignore this quote or use it to illustrate how flawed our human ignorance is. Many law breakers (which are not necessarily criminals), philosophers, icono-blasts, anarchists, and teachers would find this useful. And you may find it useful any time you encounter a law you don't like.

33)   I could be bounded in a nutshell and count myself a king of infinite space, were it not that I have bad dreams. 2.2.258-260.

"I could be locked away, cramped, stifled, and pretend that I have all the freedom in the world, except that I have bad dreams." We are not free unless we can control our thoughts, an extension of Satan's "The mind is its own place" in *Paradise Lost*. It is a great rebuttal for whenever someone says "It was just a dream."

34) What a piece of work is man!
2.2.312.

A cheeky response to anyone who says "I just don't get you," or an equally smart comment on a dapper, well-dressed man. It also could apply to oneself if the shoe fits. It is a great observation of humanities' gravest mistakes and greatest accomplishments.

35) Man delights not me-- no, nor woman neither, though by your smiling you seem to say so.
2.2.317-319.

"I don't like men right now, and don't like women either, even though your smirk seems to say I do." Hamlet is speaking to Guildernstern, one of his would-be murderers. The first part of this quote is useful when dealing with annoying neighbours or bad dates. You can also spring this entire quote when you are at a club and don't like the look of the crowd.

36) An old man is twice a child.
2.2.394.

There are several ways to interpret this
quote. One of the most popular is to take it that
an old man becomes a child again- unable to
tend to himself, soiling himself, babbling like
an idiot, etc. It easily carries over to trying to
deal with a stubborn old man who acts like a
two year-old and refuses to listen. It also
applies to old men behaving foolishly and
reflects an anonymous piece of poetry on the 7
ages of man.

Not Old enough to know better
Not Old enough to know
    Old enough to know better
    Old enough
Not Old
    Old
Not

37) Use every man after his dessert, and
who shall 'scape the whipping?
2.2.540-541.

"If we all got what we deserve, who wouldn't be punished?" This is a desperate plea for mercy before any judge, traffic officer, spouse, or tax collector. Here Hamlet is playing with Polonius, so perhaps it is meant to be taken sarcastically, but it still connects to anyone guilty, or guilt-bound by conscience.

38) Use them after your own honour and dignity; the less they deserve, the more merit is in your bounty.
2.2.542-543.

"The nicer you are to those who don't deserve it, the more noble is your service." It is more charitable to give to the especially poor and undeserving because it takes greater strength and effort. Be sure to keep this quote handy for when your kids, friends, or siblings ask you for a favour; if you do them the favour, you are so much better than they deserve you to be, so lord it over them a little bit. This quote can also encourage charity from the most Scrooge-like miser and is a great cash collector at any fundraiser, telethon, or charity event.

39) O, what a rogue and peasant slave am I!
2.2.560.

Hamlet is chastising himself for not being a man of action, and for not feeling more hot-blooded upon hearing of his father's murder. It is a heartfelt cry to use when you feel self-loathing or regret. It is also a great way to show humility before a spouse or lover when you've done something wrong, and to turn the conversation to something lighter and more humorous. Who would try outdoing this statement?

40) With devotion's visage, and pious action we do sugar o'er the devil himself.
3.1.47-49.

"By pretending to love we fool (or get sweet favours from) the devil himself." A cry for sycophants and inheritors alike, and the hallmark cry of trick-or-treaters. A great quote whenever a costume of any sort is being played in, or when someone is obviously brown-nosing in order to get ahead.

41) There's the rub.
   3.1.68.

"There's the problem," or "there's the insult." When something is craved yet unobtainable in a catch-22 sort of way, or when you are injured by insult and can't quite extract your revenge, hurl this quote. It applies to any point of contention or a specific aspect of something that gets to you. For example, if you are arguing with a waiter about your dinner, and the issue is not so much what was served, but *how* it was served to you, the rub is the poor service, which made the whole meal a bad experience. It is the same for Hamlet as he contemplates death or suicide; he could die, but the key point is he does not know what happens after death, and that issue is the big one that really makes it tough to give up life. It is the rub or the pivot that the whole issue turns on. Use this when you are bothered by anything, or the next time you are at a BBQ contest, either preparing to or taking a bite of some dry rub ribs.

42) They are the abstract and brief
chronicles of the time.
2.2.545-536.

"They are the intangible and short-lived records of the time." Another way to take it more in context is, "Their performances are the abstract, the shortened version of the big events of our days." This quote is Hamlet's recognition of how fleeting and short-lived the artistic works of actors are as he hires some to expose his uncle's guilt. Naturally, things are less brief now because of recordable media, but the sentiment is still useful. It is a nice quote to downplay the impact and importance of celebrity couples, as well as to downplay "news" in newspapers, the internet, and on TV. It is also a nice way to put an end to stupid gossip making the rounds at your workplace or dinner table.

"They are the abstract and brief chronicles of the time."

"To be or not to be - -that is the question."

43) To be or not to be-- that is the question. 3.1.56.

"To exist or not; that is the question."
These may be the most often quoted words ever
written by Shakespeare. Who has not heard
them in a thousand different uses from, "to
sleep or not to sleep?" to the apartment hunter
trying to decide if he should take apartment 2B
or not? Any word can be substituted for "be",
and they all are equally banal and funny at the
same time. Everyone sees the punch line
coming once the first 'to' comes off the lips of
the would-be punster. With it so common and
so useful, it is a good idea to have some clue as
to what this quote means.

    This quote comes as Hamlet struggles with
the decision of whether or not to kill his uncle-
father, and "Be" (yes, capital as in big "Be") a
part of this immoral world that he has found
himself in, or not. This play repeatedly presents
the issue of performance vs. being, or how to
know what people really are. Hamlet struggles
with this as he watches the world around him.
Particularly important is the example of his
mother who once seemed a devoted wife. She

now seems unfaithful for getting married so
quickly after her husband's death, but maybe
she only seemed devoted before. With his
certainty in people shaken, Hamlet feigns
madness because he needs to know what
everyone really is, not what they pretend to be.
The big question naturally is why is pretending
such a bad thing? More importantly to us, why
does Hamlet demand the truth?

Hamlet demands the truth because
seeming or trying to seem is destroying his
world. When we consider how Hamlet's
feigned insanity destroys Ophelia, we see how
caring too much about what people think can
yield tragic consequences. This is especially
true when people play others for their own
needs. Hamlet doubts the validity of
everything, even existing; it is all one big lie,
and if nothing is genuine, why pursue the lofty
goals of the world? He does not care what
others think. He is acting like a lunatic, so what
worry could he have? To be (genuine) or not to
be (genuine), that is THE question. Is existence
better than death? Maybe; maybe not. Maybe
it makes no difference. Seeming mad may be a
good "being" for him, but being is dangerous.

The players who really want to be a part of Denmark all end up dead. Polonius tries to be an intelligent courtier; Claudius tries to be his brother the king; Hamlet's own father tried to be ruler of Denmark; Rosencrantz and Guildenstern try to be important players in the court; Ophelia tries to be a faithful daughter against her own aspirations of love. All that Hamlet sees in this world is people pretending, or trying to be, and the only escape from it all is not being, or death. This death can be a figurative death, as in no more pretending, or the literal act of dying. Either way, to opt out of seeming, a person must stop existing in some sense; so Hamlet has come to the conclusion he should either be real, or die and not be at all. This is his question.

Perhaps the only answer to Hamlet's question about existence comes from the player who deals with death the most, the gravedigger; he has no pretext of being. Although he arrives much later in the play, the gravedigger (or clown) seeks the truth of existence through riddles. Through these riddles, Hamlet is finally forced to see the end of life and to know that the riddle of existence, like any true riddle, has an entirely obvious answer.

Life is essentially a brief lie about what we really are. Laugh at life, joke about it, and enjoy it in whatever role you have. Soon you will be food for worms, or being heaved out of your "final" resting place to make way for another to "be" dead in. Even death, the permanent state that will grip us all, is not a permanent state of "being" dead in the ground! Yet, this is what we all come to; only absurd impermanence is found between birth and death, and even in death, as Hamlet sees when he jokes with Yorick's skull. When he says, "tell my lady to paint an inch thick" he is not just making fun of what Yorick has become, but also of how his mother pretends to be by using makeup. Joking reveals truth; a joke is essentially a lie or a temporary false being with a happy twist on it, so a version of life itself. We are never permanent because we pretend all along the way, and since this is life, life is a joke. Anyone without a clown's approach to life will miss the riddle and miss out on life entirely.

If a man chooses to "be" he must give up critical knowledge of what life is for tragic optimism of what life can be. The man with the worst job in the world, the gravedigger, has learned to "be" a clown in a world of tragedy, filth, and death; that being came through practice and choice. Choice gives meaning to life while accepting it as absurd. In order to genuinely be, you must at first seem, or try, to be, and therein lies the absurdity; seeming is being. So the next time you find yourself asking "why?" about anything, use this quote; it is a statement of validation, humanism, existentialism, and hope. Any use, clever or not, is completely in tune with the spirit of trying to enjoy life and being unsure about what exactly that means. Elsewhere in the play, Hamlet suggests "What should a man do but be merry?" He says be, and not seem, but maybe seeming merry is good enough. Life is quite absurd, but if you can find meaning in it and share a laugh along the way, so be it.

44) To die to sleep- no more; and by a sleep to say we end the heart-ache and the thousand natural shocks that flesh is heir to.
3.1.60-63.

"By death we prevent any further unkindness or suffering on ourselves." This is Hamlet's pessimistic outlook on life and whether or not to bear it. Life for him has become so miserable that he almost cannot bear being alive. "The thousand natural shocks that flesh is heir to" is a great quote by itself. It can be used to dull the reaction to anything upsetting to one's significant other or parents, be it a new Mohawk hairstyle, a sad departure, or even passing gas.

45) Who would these fardels bear,to grunt and sweat under a weary life, but that the dread of something after death— the undiscover'd country, from whose bourn no traveller returns- puzzles the will, and makes us rather bear those ills we have than fly to others that we know not of? Thus conscience does make cowards of us all 3.1.76-83.

"Well why put up with life and persist in this tragic voyage, this suffering? We stay alive because we fear death. Fearing that the unknown after death may be worse than life makes us all cowards." Hamlet continues to ponder the mysteries and miseries of life and to wonder why we put up with life at all. His reasoning is pretty clear; no one ever comes back from that "undiscover'd country" of death, itself a useful quote for any discovery or venture. Furthermore, being self-aware, or having a conscience or consciousness, often keeps us from trying new things or taking risks.

We fear death, or risks of new actions, and so we stagnate and put up with our lives as they are. But does stagnation prevent death? There is literal death, and there is the figurative death of compromise. If we stop trying, we stop growing, and so this quote becomes relevant any time we let ourselves or our souls die just a little bit by being cowardly. This idea paraphrases some psychologists' theories in a nutshell; people would rather be miserable with familiarity than risk being happy with the unknown. Use this to encourage people to take risks, or to validate not taking a risk at all when the stakes are too high.

46) Rich gifts wax poor when givers prove
    unkind.
    3.1.101.

"Good gifts become bad gifts when the
givers turn out to not mean it." This is an
insightful line from Ophelia as she cautiously
flirts with Hamlet, and is the cry of many a
slighted fiancé or anyone who has been given
stolen property as a present. Hallmark has yet
to adopt this sentiment, but it would be great on
gift cards or in the fine print of an engagement
ring.

47) Your honesty should admit no
    discourse to your beauty.
    3.1.106-107.

"Your honesty shouldn't depend upon
your beauty" is the wider translation, but in
context it could mean "your honesty should not
change with how you want to appear to others."
If you interpret it as the latter, then it becomes a
convicting cry for politicians; no one should
change their tune to save face or because it

would make them look better. Hamlet again pushes the theme of appearance and reality, or in this case honesty, as he debates and flirts with Ophelia. This quote really means that honesty and character should come first and foremost; it's what's inside that counts. As well, this is a great phrase for anyone you know who is obsessed with appearances, or fakes their way through life.

48) If thou wilt needs marry, marry a fool; for wise men know well enough what monsters you make of them. 3.1.139-141.

This is Hamlet's timeless and completely undeserved insult to Ophelia, and perhaps all women, at the end of their debate. Change "will needs" to "must" and its meaning becomes clear. This is a unique chastisement for anyone who toys with men, either wittingly or unwittingly. Also, this quote is well used in any breakup. And if you ever have to meet with the paparazzi, have the second half of this quote ready and go on the offensive.

49) Madness in great ones must not
    unwatch'd go.
    3.1.91.

"Be careful of anyone who is powerful and
crazy." This simple assertion of Claudius is
quite prophetic considering the early half of the
20th century. It is a great quote to use when you
are accused of being mad and trying to bluff
your way to greatness. It lives in literature in
the Red Queen of *Alice in Wonderland*, and in
the real world in countless politicians, tyrants
and celebrities.

50) God hath given you one face, and
    you make yourselves another.
    3.1.145-146.

Hamlet ends his verbal assault on Ophelia
with a quick assessment of duplicity in
personality and behaviour, but it could be about
makeup. Highly applicable to anyone who
feigns personality or playacts to get their own
way. Use this before Halloween, a play, a
masquerade, or a political debate.

"God hath given you one face and you make yourselves another."

51) O, it offends me to the soul to hear a robustious periwig pated fellow tear a passion to tatters, to very rags, to split the ears of the groundlings, who, for the most part, are capable of nothing but inexplicable dumb shows and noise. 3.2.8-13.

"I hate to hear a poorly costumed fool butcher a fine piece of work in front of a crowd of dense rabble who can only notice colors and noise." Hamlet's (and probably Shakespeare's) pointed criticism of bad acting made worse by bad audiences. A wonderful commentary on Hollywood, and great for any aspiring writer whose work is rejected, or worse yet, butchered to make it pleasing to the masses.

52) Let your own discretion be your tutor. 3.2.17-18.

"Let your conscience be your guide." Hamlet again guiding actors on their performance -- maybe he was the inspiration for Jiminy Cricket? This is not a suitable guide

for most teenagers or a college bound youth,
yet it is well applied in the context that Hamlet
meant it; for actors. This is also a good way to
get a friend to stop asking you for advice since
this quote empowers and enlightens at the same
time. Say it and they will hopefully understand
that choosing will be a learning experience for
them; they should take charge of the situation
by making up their own mind.

53) Suit the action to the word, the word to
the action.
3.2.18.

"Make the actions fit the words and vice
versa." Hamlet's timeless advice for any actor,
telling them to be consistent between how they
play their part and the lines they read. It is also
a good rule of thumb for how to decide
punishment for blasphemous or swearing
children, and good advice for play by play
sports commentators.

54) I have thought some of nature's journeymen had made men, and not made them well, they imitated humanity so abominably.
3.2.35-37.

"I have thought some of the world's well-travelled beings or actors had created their own offspring, poor ones that couldn't act at that, they were so bad." This is definitely a line worth learning before you go to a community theatre production as it will probably be worth sharing afterwards. Hamlet is assessing something quite similar here; travelling performers. If you ever become a film critic, you will do well to keep this close at hand.

55) Why should the poor be flatter'd?
3.2.61-62.

"Why bother to be nice to those who do not matter?" Was Hamlet a forerunner of Ebenezer Scrooge? No, he's telling his hired actors that he is not flattering them, he is being honest in how well he thinks they can perform.

They are poor and they need his money to Survive, but he is not telling them that they are good actors just to make them feel good; he is doing it because that is his genuine opinion, flattery or intention aside. This quote makes as much sense out of context though, and as it is translated above. However, taking the words at face value has a very negative conclusion. If people are a means to an ends, who could disagree with this sentiment? This is the opposite belief of most religions, yet it is highly effective when dealing with panhandlers who refuse pennies.

56) Give me that man that is not passion's slave, and I will wear him in my heart's core, ay, in my heart of heart, as I do thee.
3.2.73-76.

"Find a man more powerful than his urges, and I will be devoted to him from deep within my heart." Hamlet is explaining his need for the play to be acted out, and that if Claudius shows no guilt, he's a rare exception among men. If Claudius is such a master of his emotions, Hamlet would love him as much as he loves Horatio. This quote out of context is true for politicians and religious leaders, and gives insight or explanation when you are trying to pick a representative in any capacity. If you need a lawyer, a partner, a business manager, or you have a friend who needs one, you would do well to find someone not controlled by emotion. And if you are a lawyer, politician, or business manager looking for a new client or job, this may be a useful quote to get you hired.

57) There's hope a great man's memory may outlive his life half a year. 3.2.135-137.

"Hopefully a great person will be remembered six months after he is dead." This is Hamlet's ironic comment on how quickly his mother remarried after his father died. Even the great are forgotten quickly after their death, although Hamlet's father may or may not have been great. It's a reminder of the brevity of life, like the morning chide of Marcus Aurelius; "remember that you too must die." This is a robust counter the next time you are heralded as a great man or great woman; chances are you'll be forgotten a few months after you're dead.

58) Where love is great, the littlest doubts are fear; where little fears grow great, great love grows there.
3.2.177-178.

"The reason I care so much is because I love so much." When your children are going out trick-or-treating and you make too much of a fuss, or you worry about anyone too much, this is a nice way to ease the tension you've caused. It helps to show that sometimes being a little bit too protective or too worried may be a good thing. Maybe this quote will help to increase some mutual understanding, maybe not, but either way it will make the reasons for your actions clearer.

59) But what we do determine oft we break. 3.2.93.

"What we really mean to do we often fail to do." This is a brilliant quote for anyone who ever swears to do anything, spoken by the King of Hamlet's play within the play, *The Mouse Trap*. It is a good spur to get you out there taking action, and a sad reminder that we often fail to do what we really mean or wish to do.

60) What should a man do but be merry? 3.2.128-129.

"When there is nothing left to do, all you can do is be merry," or, "Don't worry, be happy." This is the cry of the Hedonist, Optimist, and Epicurean all in one, and is Hamlet's sarcastic comment on his mother's happiness so soon after his father's death. Feeling hopeless? Say this. Use it to cheer up children sent to bed early, those who have no cure from sadness, or whenever "Turn that frown upside down" is a suitable sentiment.

"What should a man do but be merry?"

61) Purpose is but the slave to memory,
    of violent birth, but poor validity.
    3.2.194-195.

"Why we do something depends on our
past; usually begun with reasons powerful but
not valid or strong." You just meant to do it,
but you can't remember completely why.
Reasons in the past breed passionate actions,
but have little justification for them when you
think about them later. Questioning why you
started to do something? Then you are trying to
enslave your purpose to your memory, and
maybe you should be free of both—just do it!
If someone asks you why you did something
(it's a pity none of us knew this quote as
children), just answer with this quote. You will
be suggesting that whatever reason you could
have had, it doesn't matter now. Your grand
inquisitor will know they have been outdone,
but not quite sure why.

62) Love lead fortune or else fortune love.
    3.2.209.

"Love leads our fates, or our fates lead our love" or it could also read, "Love makes us rich, or riches make us love." Any gold-digger would find solace in this. Perhaps we do love because of status and not just because of romantic love. Perhaps there is nothing wrong with that. Asking for a pre-nup or a divorce? Here is a good line for either occasion.

63) Tis not strange that even our loves should with our fortunes change 3.2.206-207.

"It's not (or is it not?) strange that everything changes with our state in life, even love." This is the Player Queen of *The Mouse Trap* assessing the relationship between love and status. Supporting this, and using animals as an example, a female lion will become sexually receptive to the same male lion that hours before ousted her previous mate and killed her young. Keep this quote in mind the next time you hear of someone breaking off a relationship because they became rich and famous. When our fortunes and our status change, maybe it is time for a new love in our lives. Remember that in Shakespeare's time love was more of an arrangement of wealth than it was a bond of undying romance. Shakespeare plays with this idea in many of his plays, including *Measure for Measure*, *Romeo and Juliet*, and *The Taming of The Shrew*. You can use this quote to force people to play with the idea of love in their own lives and contemplate how they judge people who break up or go through a divorce. You can also use it to address gold diggers or fair-weather friends. You may love someone because they are rich, but once their fortunes changes, it may not be strange to not love them anymore.

64) Frighted with false fire!
3.2.272.

"Frightened by a farce" is Hamlet's immortal cry upon seeing his uncle foolishly scared by a play and a guilty conscience. A great quote any time someone is scared by a movie, play, fireworks, or a haunted house.

"Frighted with false fire!"

65) The lady protests too much, methinks.
3.2.236

   "She's trying too hard." This is Queen
Gertrude's often modified assessment of the
player queen in *The Mouse Trap,* Hamlet's play
within the play. It can easily be changed to
"thou doth protest too much, methinks" and
become a very practical quote indeed. It is a
powerful barb any time someone pretends to be
uninterested or too innocent and gives away
their guilt by their attempt to play it cool. Use
it to suss out a guilty party, find the truth in a
person's position, or to get those pesky
picketers off your front lawn.

66) Why, look you now, how unworthy a
    thing you make of me! You would play
    upon me; you would seem to know my
    stops; you would pluck out the heart of
    my mystery; you would sound me from
    my lowest note to the top of my
    compass: and there is much music,
    excellent voice, in this little organ; yet
    cannot you make it speak. 'Sblood, do

you think I am easier to be played on than a pipe? Call me what instrument you will, though you can fret me, yet you cannot play upon me.
3.2.371-380.

Oh the puns! "You would make me your play thing, an instrument to do what you want, make my voice reverb with spirit and soul, but you can't make me do so. I am full of song, but you can't make me sing. You can stress me out, but you can't make me stress out sounds for your pleasure." Hamlet is defending his intellect against Rosencrantz and Guildenstern, who were pressed by King Claudius to spy on Hamlet and discover his thoughts. This is an astounding quote because of the wit of the double meanings in it, and is music to the ears of anyone aware of a manipulation or poor psychology tactics. "You would play upon me" can stand alone for calling out someone who is trying to manipulate you. Ladies may want to use it coyly with a man who fancies himself a "player."

67) Now could I drink hot blood
3.2.398.

The words of Hamlet, enraged at realizing his uncle actually did murder his father. Not one to waste time, Hamlet promptly then begins to debate, argue, and delay the murder of his Uncle, although he does kill an innocent Polonius. Perhaps he would have killed Claudius if he had not found him trying to pray, thus fearing sending him to heaven, but it seems doubtful given Hamlet's skepticism. Any occasion you are mad beyond belief, this quote can instil uneasy laughter into anyone within earshot. How mad am I? "Now I could drink hot blood." Is it worse than drinking cold blood? Beasts drink hot blood, people aren't supposed to, but when anyone says this, you had better stand back. And if you say this, they had better stand back, too.

68) Now could I drink hot blood,
and do such bitter business as the day
would quake to look on.
3.2.398-400.

The same quote as above, but with a threat added onto it. Hear this spoken? Stand back. That person is dangerous, poised, *and* intelligent. Keep this handy for any occasion when you want to be taken seriously as a threat, but with just a bit of nervous humour in your words.

69) The cease of majesty dies not alone, but like a gulf doth draw what's near it with it.
3.3.15-17.

"When those who are noble stop being so, they suck into their crater of destruction all those who are close to them." This is quite a memorable quote from one of Hamlet's would-be murderers, Rosencrantz. Bad monarchs, bad politicians, bad leaders; all of them have their day. Shakespeare knew this, and knew what they do to the world around them. Any time a leader or organization drags down an entire people, don't be shocked or surprised; be austere, and quote this line from Hamlet.

70) My stronger guilt defeats my strong intent.
3.3.40.

"Try as I might I can't overcome my guilt." This quote can paint you in a bit more of a positive light by making you seem as though you have done some good in having your guilt overcome your bad intentions. Interestingly enough, the intent of praying for forgiveness saves Claudius from Hamlet murdering him on the spot. Maybe trying to appear good isn't so bad after all? This quote may be an excuse for cowardice, or for failing to carry out a foul deed, although here Claudius seems genuinely affected by his guilt. As a confession and a realization all at once, this is useful mostly to yourself, or when you need to confess. Use it when you have stopped yourself from doing something wrong or have to admit a mistake on your part. You will seem like a better person if you say you were going to do worse, but stopped yourself short and saw the error of your ways.

71) Whereto serves mercy
but to confront the visage of offence?
3.3.46-47.

"The purpose of mercy is to confront how
we look at the offense" or in other words, "We
should learn not to be offended." Mercy is not
to be given just to those who deserve it, but to
anyone who has offended. This is a great plea
before any judge or jury who cannot be moved
by reason, but who have your case close to their
heart. This is also a good way to ask for
forgiveness from a spouse or boss. You may
have done something wrong and made a
mistake, but if they can just look into their own
goodness and see that they do not need to
punish you to the fullest extent, they will be
showing genuine mercy and goodness. It is not
mercy if it is easy to do, but it is merciful of
them to be the biggest they can be and to
compensate for your most unworthy mistake.
But, in all fairness, you will also need to keep
this in mind the next time you are asked to
forgive someone who you feel really does not
deserve it.

72) Oft tis seen the wicked prize itself
     buys out the law.
     3.3.59-60.

      "The might of money often overcomes the law." What a true statement for countries pillaging other countries in the pursuit of oil. It can easily be applied to an underhanded politician breaking through the gates of law for their own purposes. No one is above the law? Not so; money talks and makes its own rules. Think of OJ Simpson, or anyone whose lawyers get them freedom when their conviction seems assured. Use this to calm someone upset at the failure of the law to do its part for them, or to succour bribes from your charges who are breaking rules.

73) Words without thoughts never to
     heaven go.
     3.3.98.

      "Actions speak louder than words." Man is saved by charity and good works; without the proofs to back up good works, you won't be able to reach heaven with your prayers. Here Claudius speaks a guilty sentiment; he is trying to pray for forgiveness and cannot. Keep this in mind when you ask for help, and use it to reply to a child's request to loan them some money; you know they don't mean to repay it, so you won't offer your heavenly charity.

74) Hoist with his own petard
      3.4.208.

"Killed by his own sword" although the more literal translation would be "blown into the air with his own bomb." A petard was an explosive used in the French army at the time. Hamlet is telling Gertrude he plans on not being a victim of Rosencrantz and Guildenstern, but rather they will be a victim of their participation in a plot against him. This is a fairly common expression, and one that you will probably notice the next time you hear it, or when you hear "live by the sword, die by the sword." You can use it whenever you outwit a competitor, beat someone at their own game, or finally get the law to help you and not hurt you.

75) O, 'tis most sweet when in one
    line two crafts directly meet.
    3.4.210-211.

"Oh, isn't it great when things come together just as you would like them to." If that is too much to ponder, just think about it as "I love it when a plan comes together." Is this a prophetic proclamation of the Titanic? Possibly, but more a general praise of the providence in all of our lives and of hard work paying off. Hamlet here is celebrating, albeit only to himself, his plans regarding his enemies working out. He has managed to get rid of Rosencrantz and Guildenstern while not implicating himself in their murder. This is a great toast to share at a wedding or anniversary, although if anyone truly knows their Hamlet, they may give you a strange look.

"O, 'tis most sweet when in one line
two crafts directly meet."

76) How shall this bloody deed be
    answered?
    4.1.16.

"What will be done about this terrible
act?" although it could easily and applicably be
translated as "How do we respond to the
mindless deeds of life?" This is the cry of
Queen Gertrude at witnessing the murder of
Polonius by Hamlet. *Hamlet, Prince of
Denmark* the play questions revenge; *The
Tempest* tells us to forgive; Queen Gertrude
raises the question of what should be the
response of the bystander. This is an
emotionally heavy quote, which is why it is so
funny to use it over a trivial matter like spilt
milk.

77) What is a man, if his chief good and market of his time be but to sleep and feed? a beast, no more. Sure, he that made us with such large discourse, looking before and after, gave us not that capability and god-like reason to fust in us unused.
4.4.33-39.

"We are meant to think and then act on those thoughts; that is the essence of being human." Hamlet is philosophizing about the meaning of being human or a man. This is great to spur a calloused or apathetic crowd to action. Do it! We are meant to think and to do, that is our purpose. According to the Tao of Jeet Kune Do, Bruce Lee once said, "To live is to express oneself freely in creation." This quote says much of the same-- we are meant to think and to act. This is what makes us human, and to do less is beastly. Use this to cure mental or physical laziness. It also defeats the quote "Ours is not to reason why, ours is but to do or die," and is worth remembering for that occasion alone.

78) So full of artless jealousy is my guilt,
    it spills itself in fearing to be spilt.
    4.5.19-20.

"I am so guilty that my jealousy cannot be
contained; it is afraid of being revealed, so it
shows itself to everyone." This is a cousin of
"Methinks thou doth protest too much." Here
the guilty party Claudius spells out his feelings
on his theft of the crown and murder of his
brother. Have a secret you can't contain?
Saying this may help you to keep it in, or it may
not. You could just say it and hope that nobody
really understands what you mean, thus
relieving the pressure of your guilt.

79) When sorrows come, they come not
    single spies, but in battalions!
    4.5.78-79.

"When trouble comes, they do not come in
ones but in the hundreds" is Claudius' timeless
comment upon seeing the insanity of Ophelia.
Some people believe that bad things happen in
threes; according to this, if you have only 3 bad

things happen to you, you are lucky, or you should expect more bad things to come. Having one of those days? Is a friend having one of those days? Here is the quote for either occasion.

80) For goodness, growing to a pleurisy,
    Dies in his own too-much.
    4.7.117-118.

"Too much goodness can be fatal; it spreads itself so much that it can choke itself, like the disease, pleurisy, does." For the record, pleurisy is similar to bronchitis or consumption, causing victims to choke on their own fluid. We are not meant to be too happy; that would be ruinous to our lives, at least that is what Claudius seems to be saying. Seem silly? Just think of how much weight you gained at that all inclusive resort or over the Christmas holidays. Eventually at a buffet, you begin to choke on the goodness or good food that is, in other situations, such a benefit to you feeling good and being happy in life. There is just too much goodness to be had, and eventually you get sick of it, or sick from it (think of travellers flu or stomach issues). It is the same with goodness and happiness in a general sense according to Hamlet. He never comes close to being overcome with happiness, but we can use this to remind ourselves that sometimes something bad needs to happen, just to keep life interesting and to make the good times seem better. Who would know the good times without the bad times to compare them to?

81) Revenge should have no bounds. 4.7.128.

The word "bounds" here means limits; change that word and you have the full meaning of Claudius' advice to Laertes. This quote has funny connotations if you have it mean "chains" or "bonds," and grim connotations when applied to POW's. It is probably best left out of the courtroom during divorce proceedings; it won't win favour from any judge or ex-partner, but it can be useful for explaining your actions.

82) Know that love is begun by time. 4.7.111.

This is the opposite of "Love at first sight." "Love either is fostered and developed by time, or changes (is begun) by what the time dictates." It is an encouraging sentiment for anyone who is rejected by someone who does not love them in return. It is also a good way out of any commitment to anything - career, relationship, journey- that has lost its savour because of too much time. However, the opposite can happen too; not enough time can prevent affection from growing. If something has not yet grown on you enough for you to want it, remember this quote. The more time you spend with it, the more time it has to genuinely grow on you. And again you can apply that idea to a relationship with someone who does not seem to like you; if you spend enough time with someone, the chance of them liking you may just increase. Think of the comedy *Overboard,* or any multitude of romantic comedies where eventually a guy or girl falls for the guy or girl they just didn't think was right.

Report Card for
Elementary Schools of Michigan

Student *Edison, Thomas*

Sept 18 *55* to January 18 *56*

Report of Achievement

Subject	1	2	3
Arithmetic		✓	
Reading		✓	
Writing	✓		
Conduct	✓		

Teacher Comments

Thomas is addled and without direction; he requires discipline if he is ever going to amount to anything. *Reverend Engle.*

To Parents

To ensure that your child is successful, we require your duty and cooperation as educators. We provide the means and ways to an education of uncompromising standards. We ask that you facilitate good citizenship and responsibility in a home environment beneficial to your child.

"Lord we know what we are, but not what we may be."

83)   Lord, we know what we are, but
       know not what we may be.
       4.5.42-43.

"We know what we are now, but not what we may become," or, "Anything is possible." This line, by the now insane Ophelia, shows the frequent wisdom of the insane in Shakespeare and perhaps in our world as well. If ever you have been told that you cannot do something, and then have done it, you know the essence of this quote in your bones. Although the exact wording has probably been changed thousands of times for thousands of different occasions, it has clear illustrations throughout history: think of Edison being told he was addled and without direction, to Michael Jordan not making his high school basketball team, and Rodney Dangerfield becoming a famous comedian in his 60's. Use this quote to give yourself strength as you reach for the stars and to inspire those around you. It is a quote with as many applications as it has inspiring examples throughout history.

84) That we would do, we should do when we would; for this 'would' changes, And hath abatements and delays as many as there are tongues, are hands, are accidents; and then this should' is like a spendthrift's sigh, that hurts by easing. 4.7.118-123.

"Just do it, before one of the millions of excuses and problems that may come gets in the way. Once you make an excuse for it, you make yourself feel better by making any excuse you can think of, thus making it less important." Here, Claudius is using this quote to move Laertes to take revenge for his fallen sister by murdering Hamlet. If there is ever anything that you say, "I would like to do it, but..." about, this quote is applicable. Just the first line and a half are great for most occasions, but the final lines will truly dazzle anyone who hears them. Essentially, it is the same as "Carpe Diem" and just about as effective when trying to get to the next base in a relationship. But if you use it when trying to psyche yourself up for something, you may just find that is quote pushes you to take that hardest first step.

Also, you should use it whenever a friend delays or procrastinates anything, such as paying taxes, asking someone on a date, confronting someone, or going out for some exercise.

85) He that is not guilty of his own death shortens not his own life.
5.1.20.

"If he didn't mean to kill himself then he did not commit murder." This is an argument over Ophelia, and as to whether or not she has committed suicide. Contextually, it is between a pair of gravediggers, or clowns as the text calls them. It is important because it sets up the gravedigger as a man who can bend words to serve his meaning, showing the duplicity of reason. Perhaps Shakespeare is predicting how legal language will lead to confusion in the modern world. It can be broadened to mean anyone who does not intentionally do harm isn't responsible, or just to divert blame at any time. Just been fired? It's not your fault; he that is not guilty of his own death ...

86) One woe doth tread upon another's heel,
    so fast they follow.
    4.7.164-165.

"One problem comes after another, and so
quickly that they are stepping on each other,"
are Queen Gertrude's immortal words to
Laertes as she tells him his sister is dead.
Having a particularly bad day? Frame it with
this statement- at least you will feel smarter for
recognizing the situation. This is not to be
quoted during a wedding procession, especially
if you are the groom awaiting the bride, but it is
very good at an endless parade or graduation.

"One woe doth tread upon another's heel, so fast they follow."

87) Nature her custom holds,
let shame say what it will.
4.7.187-188.

"Nature will do as she will, no matter what people think." Is this an excuse for passing gas in church? It could be, although here it refers to crying; Laertes is mourning the death of his sister and is crying in spite of his best intentions not to. If your body broadcasts itself beyond your control, your dog leaves waste on a neighbour's yard, or your child cries in church, here is the explanation and excuse in one go. Try as hard as you can to fight it, you cannot keep in that sneeze or prevent your body's nature from doing what it must. This is definitely a quote worth keeping close at hand.

"Nature her custom holds, shame say what it will."

88) We must speak by the card, or
    equivocation will undo us.
    5.1.139-140.

"We need to be exact, or ambiguity will prevent us from learning what we want." A stellar line by Hamlet from the infamous graveyard scene as he questions the gravedigger. This short scene is one of the most well known in all of literature and for good reason. It condenses essential questions about life, death, and the meaning of everything in between into a quick series of riddles, questions, and arguments. It also points to the ambiguity of existence, and thus, the Socratic ambiguity of what we say, and what we actually mean. Have you ever had to deal with a lawyer, insurance adjuster, or poor translator? If so, you genuinely know the meaning of this phrase, which is to use your words precisely. It is applicable to blackjack and is a common legal strategy. "What do you mean by sexual relations?"

89) Alas, poor Yorick! I knew him,
Horatio: a fellow of infinite jest, of
most excellent fancy: he hath borne me
on his back a thousand times; and now,
how abhorred in my imagination it is!
My gorge rims at it. Here hung those
lips that I have kissed I know not how
oft. Where be your gibes now? Your
gambols? Your songs? Your flashes of
merriment, that were wont to set the
table on a roar? Not one now, to mock
your own grinning? Quite chap-fallen?
Now get you to my lady's chamber, and
tell her, let her paint an inch thick, to
this favour she must come; make her
laugh at that.
5.1.185-197.

"He made me laugh, he carried me
piggyback many times, we bonded and were so
close! And now, where are the laughs, the
humour, the smiles, the jokes? What would
you say about this, would you laugh at
yourself? For a last prank go to my mother's
room and tell her to put on an inch of

makeup, because in the end, this is what we all end up as, so let her in on the joke." This is one of the most famous quotes in Hamlet, well, at least the first few words are. It is his lamentation and pondering of life spurred by finding the skull of a court jester he knew being tossed up out of the grave and onto the earth with no regard. It is also a point where Hamlet is forced to confront something that is not just an appearance; the reality is we all die. Thus, this quote beautifully sums up Hamlet's chief problem in the play-- believing in a philosophical disposition, in anything really, in the face of a tragic, short life.

We may paint ourselves one way or another, both literally with makeup and figuratively with our actions, but in the end we all end up the same; dead and buried in the ground, forgotten and as nothing of significance to anyone around. If you find this prospect depressing you are not alone. But you can still use this quote to have a few laughs. When do you use this quote? Whenever you see a skeleton or hear of a clown dying. Or the next time you have a thanksgiving dinner and are face to face with the turkey itself.

90) To what base uses we may return 5.1.204.

"What low and degrading states of being we may end up as." My younger brother was a good musician, but every school concert or production ended up with him playing bass guitar. He really didn't care for this quote when it sprouted up after a performance. In context, this quote from the character Hamlet translates into "We are all born from dust, and all can end up as little more when it's all said and done." It is Hamlet commenting on finding the skull of his beloved court jester, Yorick. "Ashes to ashes, dust to dust" has almost the same meaning. Use this quote when performing manual labour, cleaning dirty diapers, attending a funeral, or whenever you have to stoop low to get a job done.

91) Why may not the imagination trace the noble dust of Alexander till 'a find it stopping a bung-hole?
5.1.205-206.

"Why could you not imagine how the body of Alexander the great would turn to soil, then tree, and then become a plug for a barrel of beer?" Here Hamlet is waxing poetic in the graveyard scene as he contemplates death and what is in store for us all. We stop being and then become dirt underfoo,t and then dirt clogging a hole in a barrel or the bung-hole in a barrel. Depending on who you listen to and how modern of an interpretation you want to give it, a bung-hole may even mean someone's anus. If that is the interpretation, then the meaning becomes "The greatest of us becomes toilet paper for paupers." This is a great way to make an apology for calling someone petty, or insignificant, or a piece of crap. If they pause to think about it, you have not besmirched them in any way. Why not? "Well, think about it, really we all are. Why may not the imagination…"

92) Sweets to the sweet
    5.1.245.

Is this a genuinely affectionate
compliment or a sarcastic spur? It all depends
on how you decide to emphasize and use it.
Here it is Gertrude's genuine sentiment as she
scatters flowers over the dead Ophelia,
mimicking some of Ophelia's words earlier in
the play. Some favourite occasions for this
quote; Valentine's day, feeding a newborn, and
giving Easter eggs.

93) Our indiscretion sometimes serves us
    well, when our deep plots do pall; and
    that should learn us. There's a divinity
    that shapes our ends, rough-hew them
    how we will.
    5.2.8-11.

"Sometimes our impulses are a better
guide for us than our thoughts or well laid out
plans. There is a fate that works to finish our
plans, try and lay them out as we will." Whenever you make a mistake of passion, or

indiscretion, use this phrase; you'll buy some time to see how it all turns out. The entire quote is a witty explanation of fate and the subconscious' power to make us do what we cannot rationally explain; think "I've got a feeling about that number." However, only the first or last line is necessary to make your point. Use this to boost your faith in your instincts or god as in, "Fate (or god) has a plan for all of us. If I'm meant to win, I'm going to win. If not, I won't."

94) Tis dangerous when the baser nature comes between the pass and fell incensed points of mighty opposites. 5.2.60-62.

"Don't get caught in the middle of a fight." A sensible cry for any referee or sibling, although using it when needed is difficult. Hamlet is discussing the foolishness of Rosencrantz and Guildenstern trying to get involved in the battles of the court. No one is likely to heed such a cry, even when they know they should. It is better used to keep someone else out of trying to stop a quarrel than to actually stop a quarrel yourself.

95) Let a beast be lord of beasts.
    5.2.87.

Almost "Let the baby have his bottle," only with overtones of disease, corruption, and derogatory actions. Hamlet has given up on being king, or at least hasn't pursued it with any genuine interest, and this is his explanation why. Who wants to lead a rabble of vile people? A vile person. Why would you want to get involved in a turf war, bragging contest, or any of the multitude of stupid contests that people with nothing better to do get involved in? A biting comment after losing any election, contest, board game, or bid for promotion.

96) If it be now, 'tis not to come; if it be not to come, it will be now; if it be not now, yet it will come: the readiness is all: since no man has aught of what he leaves, what is't to leave betimes? Let be.
5.2.220-225.

"We try to change our lives, but in the end all things are not up to us. Things are going to either happen or not; we may as well accept our fate and enjoy it." This is a nice little taste of optimism in the face of fatalism. It sounds a lot like a story told by Irwin Barker about a fatalist who was also an optimist; when she slipped and broke her leg, she said "I'm glad I got that over with." Hamlet is still constant to his purposes; if it is his time, it is his time. If it is not, it is not, so why worry? The opening line is bound to be useful for anyone who feels the odds are stacked against them. The remainder of the lines are a humanist cheer against destiny and fortune, and a battle cry to try no matter what the fate may be. These are words of courage and hope, especially when you are buying a lottery ticket.

97) I am constant to my purposes.
5.2.202.

"I will do what I said I would." Is it wise
of Hamlet to follow through on his purposes?
Here he states he will not forfeit his duel with
Laertes, despite having a bad feeling about it.
The reader must decide if it is a bad decision
for Hamlet, and also must decide how this is to
be taken; is it a cry of foolish stubbornness, or a
cry of heroic commitment to a goal? It is useful
when you swear you know where you are going
and do not want to stop for directions, and even
more useful when your followers lose their
faith in you.

98)   I am justly kill'd with mine own
        treachery.
        5.2.308.

A wonderful cry when the tables are
turned; here Laertes laments his defeat by the
poison he meant to kill Hamlet with. This is
great during board games, sports defeats, or in
political elections.

99)   The foul practice hath turn'd itself on
        me.
        5.2.318-320.

"I have reaped what I sewed." Laertes
owns up to trying to murder Hamlet, and admits
that his trying to kill Hamlet has led to his own
death. The theme of the validity of revenge and
what that leads to again arises in this play.
Change the spelling of foul, and it is exactly
what Colonel Saunders would say if he ended
up covered in batter and deep-fried. This quote
is excellent whenever irony rears its ugly head,
or when you have been held to your word and
you didn't want to be.

"The foul practice hath turn'd itself on me."

100) Was't Hamlet wrong'd Laertes? Never
   Hamlet. If Hamlet from himself be
   ta'en away, and when he's not himself,
   does wrong Laertes, then Hamlet does
   it not, Hamlet denies it. Who does it,
   then? His madness.
   5.2.234-238.

"If I was out of my mind when 'I' did it,
then 'I' am not really responsible, but my
insanity did it, not 'I'." Is this where our
modern interpretation of legal insanity comes
from? It seems like a sound argument and the
logic of it is clear to any layperson. If you are
given to passions or rage, then this quote is
yours for the keeping. If you ever have to deal
with monthly madness, you can turn it to your
advantage; when you have it, or when you have
to deal with your partner having it, say you are
not responsible. If you are arguing with
someone who does suffer from monthly
madness, say that you aren't arguing with them,
but rather their madness.

101) Horatio, I am dead: thou livest; report me and my cause aright to the unsatisfied.
5.2.339-342.

"Horatio, I am a dead man; tell everyone who needs to know what really happened." This is the dying request of Prince Hamlet spoken to Laertes. It is great for any melo-dramatic moment in the household or workplace. One thematic idea of it is that he asks Horatio to "report my cause aright". Hamlet is not saying "a'ight" or "alright" but rather that he wants the report of what happened, and the reason why he has been acting so strange for so long properly clarified and justified, or reported right. He wants Horatio to clear his name and tell everyone the truth about his situation, a final attempt to show that there is a difference between the way we seem to others, and the way we actually are. Use that segment any time you are being spoken about; ask people who misquote you or mistake your meaning to "report your cause aright". Who would argue with such a request?

102) Good night, sweet prince; flights of
angels sing thee to rest.
5.2.359-361.

   Such a cliche! It has tragic overtones in
the play; Horatio, Hamlet's best friend in the
play, speaks this line to him as Hamlet dies of
poison. They are a cry and a prayer for anyone
who has lost a loved one or friend, and wishes
the purest symphony of love to lay them to rest.
On a less somber note, I had a friend who lived
above a noisy bar. He cracked a special smile
on his face when I said this to him one night.
You can use it when your children keep asking
for just one more bedtime story.
   Of course there is the off chance that you
are reading this in bed, hoping for a good sleep
and something like wisdom from Shakespeare
to sing you off to bliss. If that is the case,
dream of beautiful music and relax knowing
that the greatest author of all time would love
you using his words to shape your dreams.
After all, "We are such stuff as dreams are
made on; and our little life is rounded with a
sleep." (*The Tempest*, 4.1.146-148.)
   Adieu. Adieu. Adieu.

"Flights of angels sing thee to thy rest."

Practice Test # 1: Be Ready!
Sharpen your wit.

Now you can practice your wit! Read these and test yourself. Different answers may fit the scenario, depending upon your intention. However, there is a best answer that truly reflects both the meaning and the context of the scenarios. If you dislike these, know that love is begun by time.

1) You've been speeding. A police officer pulls you over; he seems on the fence about giving you a ticket, and pauses after saying "usually, it's a $100 fine." You say;

   A) Horatio I am dead
   B) The foul practice hath turned itself on me
   C) Use each man after his dessert and who shall 'scape the whipping
   D) To speed or not to speed
   E) I am constant to my purposes

2) You're late for a dinner date and need an excuse or an explanation. What should you say?

   A) I am constant to my purposes

   B) We defy augury

   C) He that is not guilty of his own death shortens not his own life

   D) That we would do, we should do when we would

   E) Whereto serves mercy but to confront the visage of offence?

3) A friend wants you to give him a ride. You say:

   A) With devotion's visage, and pious action we do sugar o'er the devil himself

   B) My stronger guilt defeats my strong intent

   C) To be or not to be

   D) Why, look you now, how unworthy a thing you make of me! You would play upon me; you would seem to know my stops

   E) O, what a rogue and peasant slave am I

4) You have to take a long drive and you want your friend to come along to keep you company. You say to him:

A) There's the Rub
B) There is nothing either good or bad, but thinking makes it so
C) Nature cannot choose his origin
D) This above all- to thine own self be true
E) Any of the above

5) You have given away your spouse's favourite shirt at a garage sale. To quell their anger you say:

A) Tis unmanly grief
B) Foul deeds will rise
C) The apparel oft proclaims the man
D) There's the rub
E) I know not seems

6) A client asks your opinion on the upcoming election, hoping to get closer to you. You despise their favourite candidate but worry about how they would take the news. You say:

A) Sweets to the Sweets
B) Though this be madness, yet there is method in't.
C) An old man is twice a child
D) Use each man after his dessert and who shall 'scape the whipping

7) You have forgotten what section you parked in. Your companion is getting impatient, so you say:

A) To be or not to be
B) Though this be madness, yet there is method in't
C) Nature cannot choose his origin
D) Your honesty should admit no discourse to your beauty
E) Madness in great ones must not unwatch'd go

8) You see a female friend getting ready for a date with someone that she dislikes. You say:

A) Your honesty should admit no discourse to your beauty
B) With devotion's visage, and pious action we do sugar o'er the devil himself
C) Let your own discretion be your tutor
D) But what we do determine oft we break
E) Any of the above

9) You are walking down the street and a charity worker stops you to ask you for money. You say:

A) Purpose is but the slave to memory, of violent birth, but poor validity
B) Tis not strange that even our loves should with our fortunes change
C) The foul practice hath turned itself upon me
D) That we would do, we should do when we would
E) Our indiscretion sometimes serves us well

10) A young boy refuses to eat his dinner until you explain to him it is something he actually likes, so you say:

A) My stronger guilt defeats my strong intent
B) Our indiscretion sometimes serves us well
C) The cease of majesty dies not alone, but like a gulf doth draw what's near it with it
D) Suit the action to the word, the word to the action
E) Youth to itself rebels.

Practice Test # 2 :
Be Good and Ready
Practice maketh a ready woman or man

The more you practice, the sharper your wit. Make your wit good and strong, ready for use at a moment's notice and in any situation possible so that you can show off. Remember, "all the world's a stage".

1) A friend of yours keeps you waiting 20 minutes on a lunch date. You are very upset so you say:

A) Now could I drink hot blood
B) But what we do determine oft we break
C) Whereto serves mercy but to confront the visage of offence?
D) Why, look you now, how unworthy a thing you make of me!
E) That we would do, we should do when we would

2) You have a presumptuous waiter who gives you bad service. You leave a bad tip with a note saying:

A) Oft tis seen the wicked prize itself buys out the law
B) Words without thoughts never to heaven go
C) Sweets to the sweet
D) Use each man after his dessert
E) The foul practice hath turn'd itself on me

3) You are tired and don't feel like doing the dishes, but know you had better. To motivate yourself you say:

A) Thus conscience does make cowards of us all
B) To persevere in obstinate condolement is a course of impious stubbornness
C) O, what a rogue and peasant slave am I!
D) That we would do, we should do when we would
E) Use each man after his dessert

4) You are at the dentist and he asks you how often you have been flossing your teeth. You feel guilty and so reply with:

A) Our indiscretion sometimes serves us well
B) Youth to itself rebels
C) To be honest, as this world goes, is to be one man pick'd out of ten thousand
D) To floss or not to floss
E) Any of the above

5) One of your best friends has just announced their engagement to their longtime partner. You say:

A) To be honest, as this world goes, is to be one man pick'd out of ten thousand
B) Virtue itself 'scapes not calumnious strokes
C) To persevere in obstinate condolement is a course of impious stubbornness
D) To what base uses we may return
E) None of the above; this is your friend.

6) You see a Lady Gaga poster while walking with your mother. She cannot understand the appeal so you say:

   A) There are more things in heaven and earth, Horatio, than are dreamt of in your philosophy
   B) Madness in great ones must not unwatched go
   C) Youth to itself rebels
   D) We know what we are, but not what we may be
   E) Any of the above

7) You see another Lady Gaga poster while walking with your father. He cannot understand the appeal so you say:

   A) Let a beast be lord of beasts
   B) The chariest maid is prodigal enough if she unmask her beauty to the moon
   C) The apparel oft proclaims the (wo)man
   D) to thine own self be true
   E) Any of the above

8) A friend of yours finally went on a date with someone you knew was perfect for her and she now is in love. You say:

A) Tis not strange that even our loves should with our fortunes change
B) Hoist with his own petard
C) The lady protests too much, methinks
D) O, 'tis most sweet when in one line two crafts directly meet

9) You are having a terrible day. A friend asks you what is wrong so you say:

A) Tis not strange that even our loves should with our fortunes change
B) Where love is great, the littlest doubts are fear; where little fears grow great, great love grows there
C) But what we do determine oft we break
D) When sorrows come, they come not in single spies but in battalions

10) A neighbour's toddler keeps running away
so you tell her parents:

- A) I could be bounded in a nutshell and count myself a king of infinite space, were it not that I have bad dreams
- B) Madness in great ones must not unwatch'd go
- C) My stronger guilt defeats my strong intent
- D) Why should the poor be flatter'd?
- E) Those friends thou hast, and their adoption tried, grapple them to thy soul with hoops of steel

Practice Test # 3
Be ready for all occasions

Do you feel like it is possible to be ready for all occasions, to be an expert at quoting Shakespeare? Of course it is! Remember, we know what we are, but not what we may be.

1) You make dinner and despite Martha Stewart's instructions it turns into a disaster. You say:

A) It was not to be
B) Our indiscretion sometimes serves us well
C) There's the rub
D) My stronger guilt defeats my strong intent
E) Any of the above

2) You are walking your dog and he stops to mark the leg of a priest. You feel terrible but find it quite funny, so you say:

A) Nature her custom holds, shame say what it will
B) What should a man do but be merry?
C) Our indiscretion sometimes serves us well
D) That we would do, we should do when we would
E) Any of the above

3) Your family dislikes new types of food. To encourage some adventure you say:
A) Know that love is begun by time
B) Why, look you now, how unworthy a thing you make of me!
C) What is a man, if his chief good and market of his time be but to sleep and feed?
D) My stronger guilt defeats my strong intent
E) Suit the action to the word, the word to the action

4) Your best friend is sick and in hospital. To cheer her up you say:

   A) My stronger guilt defeats my strong intent
   B) The cease of majesty dies not alone, but like a gulf doth draw what's near it with it
   C) Here's hope a great (wo) man's memory may outlive his(her) life half a year
   D) What should a man do but be merry?
   E) Who would these fardels bear...

5) You are out on a date and you have forgotten your wallet. To ease the tension you say:

   A) What should a man do but be merry?
   B) O, what a rogue and peasant slave am I!
   C) With devotion's visage, and pious action we do sugar o'er the devil himself
   D) Suit the action to the word, the word to the action
   E) Any of the above

6) Your friend fails an important exam. You
want to condole them and so you say:

   A) Oft tis seen the wicked prize itself buys
   out the law
   B) God hath given you one face, and you
   make yourselves another
   C) Suit the action to the word, the word to
   the action
   D) That we would do, we should do when
   we would
   E) There's a divinity that shapes our ends,
   rough-hew them as we will

7) You bluff a win in a poker game. As you
rake in your chips you say:

   A) O, 'tis most sweet when in one line two
   crafts directly meet
   B) My stronger guilt defeats my strong
   intent
   C) Frighted with false fire!
   D) Hoist with his own petard

8) You are late on your income taxes and don't want to pay the fine. You say:

   A) Oft tis seen the wicked prize itself buys out the law
   B) That we would do, we should do when we would
   C) Foul deeds will rise, though all the earth o'erwhelm them, to men's eyes
   D) Whereto serves mercy but to confront the visage of offence?
   E) Any of the above

9) You finally have found a new job after years of trying, but your old boss wants you to stay. You say:

   A) I could be bounded in a nutshell and count myself a king of infinite space
   B) What we do determine oft we break
   C) As if increase of appetite had grown by what it fed on
   D) Oft tis seen the wicked prize itself buys out the law
   E) Any of the above

10) Your car has run out of gas and it is your fault. You say:

A) What we do determine oft we break
B) Hoist with his own petard
C) Virtue itself 'scapes not calumnious strokes
D) That we would do, we should do when we would
E) Nature her custom holds, shame say what it will

Practice Test # 4:
Suit the action to the word, the word to the action.

1) Your favourite fruit is back in season but at an extortionist price. However, you still want to buy it so you say:

   A) My stronger guilt defeats my strong intent
   B) I could be bounded in a nutshell and count myself a king of infinite space, were it not that I have bad dreams
   C) But what we do determine oft we break
   D) Our indiscretion sometimes serves us well
   E) Any of the above

2) You refuse to give up on your dream of being a famous rock musician, despite the judges on American Idol telling you there is no chance. You say to them:

A) Give me that man that is not passion's slave, and I will wear him in my heart's core
B) Oft tis seen the wicked prize itself buys out the law
C) To persevere in obstinate condolement is a course of impious stubbornness
D) I am constant to my purpose
E) Any of the above

3) Your friend keeps going on and on about the increases in taxes. To sum up her thoughts you say:

A) As if increase of appetite had grown by what it fed on
B) The foul practice hath turned itself upon me
C) Madness in great ones must not unwatch'd go
D) When sorrows come, they come not in single spies but in battalions

4) You and your family are playing a game of Risk. To inspire teamwork you say:

   A) Suit the action to the word, the word to the action

   B) Oft tis seen the wicked prize itself buys out the law

   C) Those friends thou hast, and their adoption tried, grapple them to thy soul with hoops of steel

   D) Madness in great ones must not unwatch'd go

   E) Any of the above

5) Sadly, your goldfish has died. What can you say to lighten the mood?

   A) All that lives must die, passing through nature to eternity

   B) Alas poor Yorick, I knew him, Horatio

   C) Murder most foul!

   D) What we do determine oft we break

   E) Any of the above

6) It is Christmas and you have overeaten.
You say:
   A) I could be bounded in a nutshell and
      count myself a king of infinite space
   B) As if increase of appetite had grown by
      what it fed on
   C) O, that this too too solid flesh would
      melt thaw, and resolve itself into a dew!
   D). Alas poor Yorick, I knew him, Horatio
   E) That we would do, we should do when
      we would

7) Your spouse and you are arguing over the
   correct spelling of "ridiculous". As you
   make a wager about the answer you say:

   A) Beware of entrance to a quarrel; but,
      being in, bear't that th' opposed may
      beware of thee
   B) Whereto serves mercy but to confront
      the visage of offence?
   C) Oft tis seen the wicked prize itself buys
      out the law
   D) We know what we are but not what we
      may be

8) A homeless man asks you for some
   change. You say no and add:

   A) Neither a borrower nor a lender be
   B) Now could I drink hot blood
   C) Nature cannot choose his origin
   D) I do not set my life at a pin's fee
   E) Doubt truth to be a liar, but never doubt
   I love

9) A friend tells you of a great investment
   opportunity which unfortunately turns out
   to be a timeshare. As the presentation drags
   on you say to the salesman:

   A) But what we do determine oft we break
   B) This above all- to thine own self be true
   C) Neither a borrower nor lender be
   D) More matter, with less art
   E) Whereto serves mercy but to confront
   the visage of offence?

10) You go out for dinner with a few friends and one of them suggests a wine that you cannot stand. You say:

A) Why, look you now, how unworthy a thing you make of me!
B) Sweets to the Sweet
C) Know that love is begun by time
D) Why may not the imagination trace the noble dust of Alexander till 'a find it stopping a bung-hole?
E) any of the above

Answer Key

Quiz # 1
1) C, D 2) E 3) D, B 4) B,D 5) E,B
6) D 7) A,B 8) D,E 9) A,B 10) E,D

Quiz # 2:
1) D,C 2) D,E 3) D,A 4) C,D 5) E
6) D,A 7) E 8) D,A 9) D 10)E,A

Quiz # 3:
1) B,A 2) A,E 3) A,E 4) D,E 5) B,A
6) E, A 7) E 8) D,E 9) B,D 10) C,D

Quiz # 4:
1) D 2) D,A 3) A 4) C 5) C
6) C 7) A 8) A 9) D 10) A

Illustration and Photo Credits:

Alex Kleider:
18, 24, 32, 34, 35, 40, 58, 70, 78, 82, 92, 104, 119.

Ben Nelson:
99, 122, 150, 152.

Paul Nelson:
21, 42, 44, 46, 59, 108.

Additional Titles for the "What Would Shakespeare Say" series coming soon:

Shakespeare's Why: The Philosopher's Shakespeare
Shakespeare the Shrink: Shakespeare and Psychology
A Good Wit: The Businessman's Shakespeare
Woe is Me: The Tragic Shakespeare
Heaven and Earth: The Religious Shakespeare
Be Merry: The Optimist's Shakespeare
A Gallant Creature: Shakespeare Speaks of Womyn
Meant to be: Shakespeare and Love
Things Done Well: The indispensable Shakespeare
Overdone: More Indispensable Shakespeare

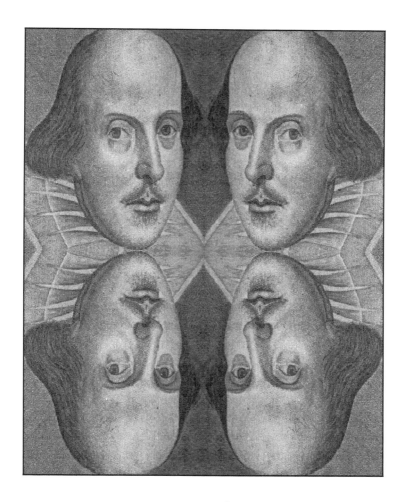

$2B^2$

About the Illustrators

Paul Nelson

Paul Nelson is Ben Nelson's older brother. He is as close as kin and more than kind and helpful when it comes to redoing illustrations. He has a wonderful wife, choice child, joyful job designing databases, and achieves his aspirations by alliteration. He has also written several films and screenplays produced for TV.

Alex Kleider

Alex Kleider is an illustrator, designer, and film maker based out of Vancouver, BC. As pictures are worth a thousand words, his work is best understood at http://www.kleiderstudios.com/

About the Author

Ben Nelson is an English teacher and a professional wrestler. He was briefly a competitor for WWE and currently competes in Canada as Nelson Creed, The Battling Bard. He enjoys using Shakespeare's words to educate and irritate wrestling fans. Ben graduated from Simon Fraser University with an English Major, Philosophy Minor, and a teaching certification. He shares his only and second-best bed with his girlfriend, Jessica, and his dog, Louis, a Maltese-poodle cross.

Ben Nelson

Bibliography

Goddard, Harold C. *The Meaning of
Shakespeare Volume 1.* Chicago: University
of Chicago Press, 1951.

Shakespeare, William. *The Tragedy of Hamlet
Prince of Denmark.* Eds. Sylvan Barnet and
Edward Hubler. New York: Penguin
Books, 1987.

For more practice quizzes, books, and fun seek:

www.whatwouldshakespearesay.com

and find us on Facebook

Made in the USA
Charleston, SC
10 January 2014